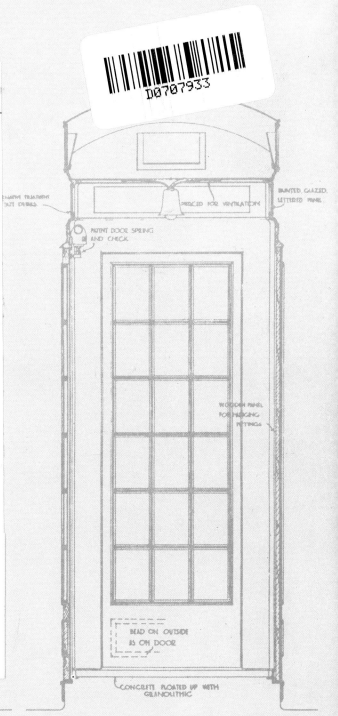

REQUIEM
FOR A RED BOX

REQUIEM FOR A RED BOX

JOHN TIMPSON

PHOTOGRAPHS

NEIL McALLISTER
VAL CORBETT

PYRAMID BOOKS

First published in 1989 by Pyramid Books,
an imprint of The Hamlyn Publishing Group Limited,
a division of The Octopus Publishing Group,
Michelin House, 81 Fulham Road, London SW3 6RB

ISBN 1-855-10008-8

Printed and bound in Great Britain by Collins, Glasgow

CONTENTS

A Paean to the Postmaster . . .

In 1924, the Postmaster-General held a competition to produce a new design for the public telephone kiosk. Sir Giles Gilbert Scott was approached and produced the 'red box' which we are so familiar with today. The judges took one look at it and went singing and dancing into the streets!

Kiosk to Kocktail Kabinet . . .

In 1985, the incipient British Telecom pronounced the death sentence on all existing kiosks. Away were to go the sacred red boxes and in were to come an assortment of booths, semi-kiosks and canopies. There was uproar. But the red-box has life in it yet!

Smithfield Market, London

RISE OF THE RED PHONE BOX

I feel a certain sympathy for Sir Giles Gilbert Scott. Here was a distinguished architect, grandson of the man who dreamed up St Pancras Station and the Albert Memorial, and chosen to design a remarkable variety of famous public buildings, from Liverpool's Anglican Cathedral to Battersea Power Station, from Cambridge University Library to Waterloo Bridge. When the House of Commons was rebuilt after the war, he was the man they sent for.

Yet, for the man in the street – and I mean that literally – what is his best-known legacy to the nation? A red box . . . . But it is only to be expected. For half a century Scott's telephone kiosks, 76,500 of them, have been a part of our lives. For anyone born since the war it has been impossible to visualise a Britain without them.

I doubt if many people think of them as architectural masterpieces. We do not pause to look for the reeded Grecian surround to the door, we do not stand back to admire how the segment-headed pediments are elided with the frieze. We might not even recognise a segment-headed pediment if it tapped us on the shoulder. A phone box is a place to make a phone call, and we are less interested in whether the roof was copied from a dead architect's tomb than whether there is life in the phone itself. Because the kiosk generally merges so well with its surroundings, we notice it even less.

There is nobody around today who can remember life before kiosks; the first ones were authorised by the Postmaster-General in 1884. But they were nothing like Scott's red boxes, and although it may be heresy to say so, some of them looked a lot more fun.

In those days there was no monopoly in the telephone service. Rival companies competed aggressively for business in any way they could, and one way was to provide call offices on busy sites. They had various ideas for making them look attractive, welcoming, even cosy. The local authorities had their ideas too. It all added to the confusion.

The biggest company, which gradually absorbed its main rivals, was called rather grandly the National Telephone Company. It was by no means national; only seventy-five towns had access to the telephone system, and only the better-off in those towns had telephones. But the phone box launched the Telephone Revolution – it brought the phone to the people.

'The National Telephone Company beg to intimate,' they announced obsequiously – there was still some competition in 1884 – 'that they are now empowered by Licence from the Postmaster-General to open "CALL OFFICES", where Any Person not a Subscriber may converse with any Subscriber to the Exchange System within a radius of Six Miles on payment of a Fee of Threepence for Three Minutes' conversation, and One Penny for each additional Minute . . .'

This was not the bargain it may have looked, and the National Telephone Company had good reason to be obsequious. The Sheffield Telephone Exchange Company, for instance, offered three minutes' chat for only tuppence, and emergency calls to the Fire Brigade 'or for calling a Cab or Medical Man in cases of accident' were free of charge.

However the National Telephone Company must have done their sums better, or perhaps they had prettier call boxes to offset the extra penny. The opposition gradually folded; only the Kingston-upon-Hull company survived, and it functions independently to this day.

By 1907 the N.T.C. had nearly eight thousand call offices bearing the company's insignia, a blue bell. The earliest ones were fairly basic, somewhere between a sentry box and a workman's hut. One of these was installed on Thorpe Station in Norwich, a wooden box with leaded windows and overhanging eaves like a tiny Swiss chalet. 'National Telephone Service', announced the sign on the roof. Rather less encouragingly, 'Trunk Calls Not Available' was written on the door. The call box justified its existence within a week – and gave the telephone company a wonderful publicity story.

On a Saturday night in February, 1907, a labourer was rescued from drowning in the freezing waters of the nearby River Wensum. He was close to expiring, but the newly-installed public telephone was used to summon a horse ambulance and his speedy transfer to hospital almost certainly saved his life.

Kiosk No. 1, Lake District

Other boxes did not have such a dramatic launch, but their mere appearance was enough to attract attention. Blackburn, at that time anxious to preserve any vestiges of a rural atmosphere, acquired a six-sided rustic arbour with ornamental log walls, leaded light windows and a wooden roof surmounted inexplicably by two large balls. Inside there was not only a telephone but an electric light, a clock provided by Blackburn Corporation, and a table and seats. It proved to be a little too luxurious. Soon after it was opened, four gentlemen of no fixed abode were found to be seated in it, enjoying a smoke and a game of cards. They were rapidly removed – and so were the table and seats.

At the other extreme, telephone boxes in dockland areas were unlovely objects made of galvanised iron, while High Holborn in London had a Parisian-style kiosk made of cast iron, with advertisements on the near-circular walls and a high domed roof. This was run by an attendant who lurked inside until a customer knocked on the door. Then he took the money, got the number, and stood outside until the call was over. One hopes he was issued with a company umbrella.

Other boxes had coin-operated doors or required pennies to be put in the apparatus – 'bent or battered coins must not be used'. The operator advised you when to insert them, and it was as well not to jump the gun; Button B had yet to be invented.

What had been invented, even in those days, was the telephone box vandal. The first recorded case was in 1907, when a Mr Samuel Wartski tried to smash open the coinbox of a kiosk in Bishopsgate Street in the City. He claimed he had put in his tuppence but the operator failed to hear and refused to connect him, whereupon Mr Wartski attacked the box with a chisel. However, he did not succeed in penetrating it, which indicates that the National Telephone Company were strong on security, even if they employed deaf operators.

Mr Wartski did nineteen shillingsworth of damage, to no avail. The magistrate apparently sympathised. 'These telephones are frequently very troublesome and annoying to those who use them,' he observed, and only fined him a shilling, though there were two guineas' court costs. The telephone company emerged with a rather tarnished image and a repair bill for nineteen shillings.

Graffiti on the white-painted surfaces inside the boxes was another early problem, and in 1912 the Postmaster General

Unsuccessful designs submitted for the 1924 design competition

approved the optimistic idea of providing scribbling pads for customers to make notes on. All that happened was the customers stole the pads and continued to scribble on the walls. A more effective solution was to varnish the walls instead. But in that same year, 1912, there was a development which had a much greater impact on the public phone box than the graffiti-writers' pencils or even Mr Wartski's chisel. The Post Office took over Britain's telephone network, and discussions began on a standard call-box design for the whole country.

The idea proved surprisingly unpopular. Places like Blackburn still liked their rural arbours, Holborn seemed to have grown accustomed to its Parisian flavour, the docklands were resigned to their galvanised iron. And local authorities were not keen on having their pavements cluttered up with more kiosks anyway.

Before the matter could be resolved the First World War began and designers turned their attention to tanks rather than telephone boxes. It was not until three years after the war ended, in 1921, that the Post Office's first standard kiosk appeared on the streets. They did not invent a catchy name for it, nor indeed for its successors. They just called it the KI.

Some experts have been scathing about the K1: 'essentially Edwardian in conception, a crude and old-fashioned design for the 1920s'. I think it looked delightful. It was a reinforced concrete version of the old wooden boxes, but smartened up with a little wrought ironwork on the roof above the 'TELEPHONE' signs, culminating in a quite unnecessary but rather dashing spear. Dr Who, I think, would have settled for it quite happily.

But it did not catch on, particularly in London where it would have brought in the most revenue. There were ninety-nine local authorities to negotiate with in the London area ranging from the City Corporation to parish councils, and most of them apparently disliked telephone kiosks in general and the K1 in particular. The Ministry of Transport also regarded them more as a traffic hazard than a public amenity. In the five years after the K1 was introduced, only 180 of them were installed in the capital. Elsewhere they were received a little more kindly, and it reached the stage when K1s were being produced and installed at the rate of fifty a month. But by then its days were already numbered. The K2 had gone into production too – the brainchild of the architect Sir Giles Gilbert Scott.

Unsuccessful designs submitted for the 1924 design competition

The first competition to find a new design, organised by the Metropolitan Boroughs Joint Standing Committee, produced kiosks with crests on, kiosks with crowns on, and kiosks with knobs on, but nothing really original. It was decided to try again, this time inviting three established and respected architects who had not bothered to enter before. Sir Robert Lorimer produced a near-K1 with a pagoda roof. Sir John Burnet produced another near-K1 with a glass dome. Sir Giles Gilbert Scott produced the K2.

Perhaps Scott had an advantage over the others – he was used to competitions. When he was only twenty-one he produced the winning design for Liverpool Cathedral. Now, at forty-three, after specializing for years in churches, he turned his mind to kiosks. He produced the 'red box' which, with some modifications, we are so familiar with today. The judges took one look at it and ran singing and dancing into the streets.

There were various reasons for their delight. To an architect, so I am assured, it is 'a distillation of the essence of Classicism'. It has the right proportions, the right projections, the right decorations. It has been suggested unkindly that Scott cribbed the design of the roof from the tomb of another notable architect, Sir John Soane, but

his devoted admirer Gavin Stamp, chairman of the Thirties Society and undisputed Champion of the Red Box, spurns such an unworthy thought. 'A dome above segmental curves is in fact a logical solution to the geometrical problem of designing a sculptural termination to a square pillar when a flat top is not suitable,' he points out sharply. We should have known that.

But apart from the architectural merits of the K2 there was its practical value. It was built of cast iron with a teak door and a concrete base, and the window panes were small and strong. It was in fact a very difficult structure to damage, which was good news for the Post Office. It was also rainproof, draughtproof and very nearly soundproof, which was good news for the customer. And it was easy to spot but not offensively obtrusive, at least in urban surroundings, which was good news for everybody. Well, nearly everybody. Some provincial areas still preferred their own variations. Eastbourne, for instance, still insisted on retaining two K1 kiosks which they had adorned with thatched roofs, absurdly out of proportion and making them look, in the words of a contemporary critic, 'a cross between a Chinese pagoda and a mushroom'.

The winning design. Sir Giles Gilbert Scott's plans and original wooden mock-up now in Burlington House, Piccadilly

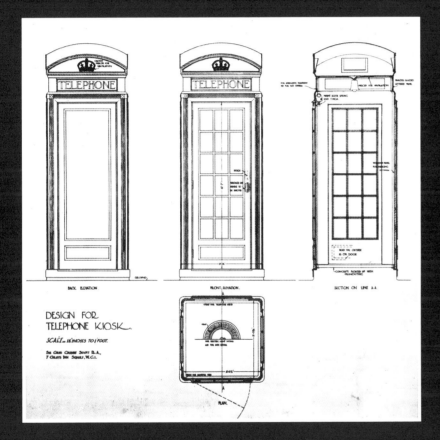

DESIGN FOR
TELEPHONE KIOSK.

SCALE 1½ INCHES TO 1 FOOT.

SIR GILES GILBERT SCOTT R.A.
7 GRAY'S INN SQUARE, W.C.1.

BACK ELEVATION

FRONT ELEVATION.

SECTION ON LINE A-A.

PLAN.

So while the K2 was put into production at £35 14s a time the K1, much cheaper at £13, continued to be widely used outside London; over six thousand were still in operation ten years later. The thatched pagoda-mushrooms at Eastbourne were not replaced until 1936. But today only five K1 kiosks are listed. Two are in museums, the others in Hull, on Ray Mill Island at Maidenhead, and at Bembridge on the Isle of Wight.

Meanwhile the K2 made its debut in 1926 in Kensington and Holborn, replacing that Parisian-style kiosk with its attendant; one hopes he was pensioned off to a comfortable and draught-free retirement. In the next eight years 1700 K2s were operating in London and other major cities. But Sir Giles and the Post Office were not resting on their kiosks. The K2 did not go from strength to strength, it went from K2 to K6, via Kiosks 3, 4 and 5.

The K3, which he was asked to design in 1927, was intended for upmarket sites, in rural areas as well as towns. It was supposed to look a little more elegant and refined. So Sir Giles switched from cast iron to concrete, made some minor adjustments to the design to pretty it up, and instead of painting it red he left it a light stone colour to merge more with its surroundings.

It was one of those projects which look good on the drawing-board but turn out to have problems in practice. The concrete kiosks were difficult to transport without breaking. If they did arrive in one piece then after a few weeks of average British weather the concrete began to crack and the paint began to peel. They also proved difficult to keep clean.

The Post Office gamely stood by Sir Giles and produced twelve thousand of his new K3s, mostly for rural areas. But perhaps it is an indication of their comparative fragility that by 1988, when there were over two hundred listed K2s, there were only two listed K3s – one of them in a museum and the other in the equally protective surroundings of the Parrot House at London Zoo.

Meanwhile the Post Office Engineering Department were having a crack at designing kiosks themselves. They took Scott's K2 and incorporated on one side of it a post office in miniature. There were two stamp machines and a letterbox displaying times of collection. Above it, on the side of Sir Giles's classical roof, they stuck a lamp. They first produced the design in 1925 and it took them five years to get it into production. They really should not have bothered. It turned out to be an embarrassing failure.

The local authorities disliked it because the bodywork had to be expanded to take the extra gadgetry, making it so bulky that it became known as the Vermilion Giant. It was difficult to find sites where it did not block the passage of pedestrians, or the view of drivers, or both. Telephone customers disliked it because when the stamp machines were used the noise blotted out their conversation. And stamp buyers disliked it because the rolls of stamps, inadequately protected from the weather, all stuck together inside the machines.

The Engineering Department placed an initial order for fifty of them. That first order proved to be the last. In the face of an outcry from shortsighted pedestrians and unsighted motorists, let alone the demands for compensation from frustrated customers, they abandoned the ill-fated K4. Just a few of them are still scattered around in the north of England, bright red reminders of all those bright red faces in the Post Office.

Nevertheless they did not give up. They produced the K5 – but its career was even briefer. The Engineering Department still had a hankering for a concrete kiosk, in spite of the snags they had already met. The accountants no doubt reminded them that

Kiosk No. 4, 'The complete miniature post office', Warrington, Cheshire

concrete was much cheaper than cast iron; the concrete K3 had only cost eleven pounds. But kiosks are designed by architects, not accountants, and although an experimental model was produced costing under nine pounds it never reached the public. Instead the Department decided to go back to the drawing-board; not theirs, but Sir Giles Scott's.

It was 1935, the year of King George V's silver jubilee. The Post Office, like the BBC, love celebrating anniversaries. They had introduced various improvements on the occasion of Queen Victoria's diamond jubilee; what could they do this time? Sir Giles provided the answer: the K6.

If you are not a phone box buff you may not immediately spot the difference between his original K2 and his new improved K6, unless they are standing side by side. Then you will see that the earlier model is a foot higher; if you have a crane and a weighbridge handy you will also find it weighs nearly twice as much.

You would have to look more closely to spot that the windows have changed. In the earlier version all the panes are the same size; the new version has

much wider panes in the middle to improve visibility, and there are eight rows of windows instead of six. Finally, you would have to look very closely indeed to discover that the doors and windows are no longer surrounded by decorative fluting, and the ventilation is provided through slots underneath the word 'TELEPHONE' instead of through holes pierced in the crowns on the roof.

The Engineering Department had a hand in the new kiosk too, but wisely they left the exterior design entirely to Scott and concentrated on the internal fittings. They produced a new apparatus in black and chrome, featuring 'A' and 'B' buttons. A new catch-phrase entered the language: 'Press Button B and get your money back'. And for the first time the Post Office gave a phone box a name as well as a number, albeit a rather obvious one: the Jubilee Kiosk.

With the arrival of a kiosk which was going to be installed throughout the countryside as well as the cities, the Post Office decided that its colour should be universal too. Urban kiosks had long since become 'Post Office red'; it was decreed that rural kiosks should be painted red too.

Left *Kiosk No. 6 or 'Jubilee', 1936*
Above *'Press button B and get your money back'*

Inevitably there were protests. Many country communities argued that a red box would be an eyesore in the midst of green fields or black-and-white timbered cottages.

It was resolved by the Royal Fine Arts Commission, which had approved the use of Post Office red as far back as 1924. In 1939 they approved it again. It was essential, they said, that a kiosk could be easily recognised in case of emergency, in any part of the country. Some rural areas were still not convinced, but then the war intervened and the argument was suspended.

After the war the Commission agreed to take part in an experiment where six kiosks were erected in rural surroundings, painted in six different colours: red, two shades of green, two shades of grey, and black. It was a kind of kiosk-tasting. After proper deliberation they relaxed their original ruling; some areas of special scenic beauty like the Lake District could paint their kiosks dark battleship grey, so long as the glazing bars were red. Some rural rebels still held out. At Okeford Fitzpaine in Dorset, for instance, the village kiosk is still painted a defiant green. But most of us will always think of the 'red box' as red.

Scott's Jubilee Kiosk first appeared on the streets in 1936. At that time there were nineteen thousand public telephones in Britain. It went forth and mutliplied, replacing the older models in the towns, entering the villages, spreading to the remotest corners of the countryside. By the time Sir Giles died in 1960 there were sixty thousand of them, and they had gained the status of an old family friend, always available for a chat, ready to help in an emergency. Even in the remotest corners of the land they were a link with the rest of the world. They became so much a part of the British way of life that postcard manufacturers used them to typify Britain, along with Big Ben, the Life Guards and the English 'bobby'. And the Post Office themselves seemed completely hooked. Said an official spokesman: 'Our Jubilee Kiosk will stand the test of time and remain a hallmark of successful enterprise and development in the interest of our people.'

That was in 1954. Five years later they were already looking for a replacement. But for half a century, on city streets and in village squares, up Welsh mountains and by Scottish lochs, alongside busy beaches or perched on lonely moors, beneath a London office block or on top of a Cornish cliff – the red box was there . . . if only to help young innocents keep in touch with their mothers . . .

Marple, Greater Manchester

*'HALLO, MUMSY DEAR? I'M SO SORRY TO
WAKE YOU BUT I'M IN A TEENY BIT OF A
SPOT. YOU SEE WE HAD THIS REALLY
SUPER PARTY AT FREDDIE'S LAST NIGHT,
LOTS OF BUBBLY AND SO ON, AND
BEFORE I KNEW IT, IT WAS GETTING
LIGHT OUTSIDE AND FREDDIE SAID HE'D
GIVE ME A LIFT, AND WE WERE DRIVING
ALONG THE EMBANKMENT WHEN HE
STOPPED THE CAR AND REALLY BEHAVED
QUITE AWFULLY, SO I SAID I'D GET OUT
AND WALK, AND I GOT OUT AND STARTED
WALKING, QUITE EXPECTING HIM TO
APOLOGISE AND ASK ME TO GET IN AGAIN,
AND THE BEASTLY MAN JUST DROVE OFF
TOOTING HIS HORN. SO HERE I AM BY
THE ALBERT BRIDGE, AND PLEASE
MUMSY, COULD YOU WAKE UP WILSON
AND ASK HIM TO PICK ME UP IN THE
ROLLS. . .'*

Albert Bridge, London

Mount Pleasant, London

Elephant and Castle, London

HIGH
NEIGHBOUR . . .

IT TAKES QUITE A MAJOR MURAL TO
OVERSHADOW A SCOTT KIOSK, BUT THE
WILD-EYED YOUNG MAN STRUGGLING
INTO HIS CLEAN SHIRT LOOMS QUITE
MENACINGLY BEHIND THE K6, AND THE
MASSIVE CARTHORSE PULLING A
BREWER'S DRAY ALONG THE PUB WALL
MAKES THE K2 BENEATH IT SEEM
ALMOST INSIGNIFICANT.

Left *Waterways Museum, Ellesmere Port, Cheshire*   **Above** *Belsize Park, London*

Fleetwood, Lancashire

Fleetwood, Lancashire

ESTABLISHED STARS

The K6 became as familiar a feature of the urban scene as the corner pub, and took on the weatherworn and slightly grubby appearance of its surroundings. In the case of this K4, vandals hastened the process.

Left *Star and Garter, Hillgate, Stockport, Greater Manchester*
Above *Kiosk No. 4, Warrington, Cheshire*

CORNER STONE

A TIME EXPOSURE DEMONSTRATES THE
CONSTANT MOVEMENT AND CHANGE AT
A BUSY ROAD JUNCTION – BANDS OF
LIGHT LEFT BY THE PASSING CARS, THE
CHANGING TRAFFIC LIGHTS SHOWING
RED, GREEN AND AMBER
SIMULTANEOUSLY, AND IF THE
EXPOSURE HAD CONTINUED LONG
ENOUGH THEN THE FLOWERS IN THE
TUBS WOULD HAVE BLOSSOMED AND
DIED. BUT THROUGHOUT ALL THIS
IMPERMANENCE, THE K6 STANDS FIRM.

Stockport, Greater Manchester

'Hallo Mumsy, I thought I'd let you know that Freddie has apologised and he's taken me out on this lovely drive in the country. He says he knows quite the perfect place for a picnic, very quiet and secluded behind all these trees. He's calling to me now; must fly. . .'

Left *Sezincote, Gloucestershire*
Right *Thaxted, Essex*

LONGCOT   3   UFFINGTON   1
SHRIVENHAM 5   FARINGDON   6
           ASHBURY   3
WHITE HORSE HILL   1½

TELEPHONE

'MUMSY DEAR, YOU WERE ABSOLUTELY RIGHT ABOUT FREDDIE. HE WAS PERFECTLY BEASTLY AGAIN AT THE PICNIC, EVEN BEFORE I'D FINISHED THE PÂTÉ SANDWICHES. SO I WALKED OFF ACROSS THE FIELD, AND I SAW A NOTICE POINTING TO THIS TELEPHONE, AND NOW IT'S GOT VERY CLOUDY AND IT LOOKS AS IF IT'S GOING TO ABSOLUTELY POUR, AND. . . OH DEAR. MUMSY, THERE'S A MAN COMING TOWARDS ME IN A FLAT CAP AND GAITERS AND LOOKING VERY, SORT OF RURAL AND PRIMITIVE. . .'

Left *Wollstone, Berkshire*
Right *Langwathby, Cumbria*

Left *Manchester*   **Above** *The Fylde, Hambleton, Lancashire*

'Yes, Mumsy, I'm quite all right,
really. He was quite a nice man,
actually, he gave me a lift to this
village. But the place seems quite
deserted; there aren't even any
ducks on the pond; very weird. I
don't think there's much chance of
a taxi here. I'll try somewhere else.
I suppose you haven't heard
anything from that rotter
Freddie. . .'

Barrowden, Leicester

Barrow-in-Furness, Cumbria

Bottle Bank, Morecambe, Lancashire

'I SAY, MUMSY, THIS REALLY IS A VERY ODD SORT OF PLACE. SOMEBODY JUST PUT SOMETHING ON TOP OF THIS PHONE BOX, AND THERE'S THE MOST FRIGHTFUL SMELL FROM THE OTHER SIDE OF THE WALL. I THINK I REALLY HATE THE COUNTRY. BY THE WAY, ANY WORD FROM FREDDIE?'

Askham, Penrith, Cumbria

Crossdale, Cumbria

Dacre, Cumbria

48

THE HOMELY TOUCH

IT MIGHT HAVE MERELY BEEN DUMPED
THERE, BUT WHAT A NICE THOUGHT IF
SOMEBODY PROVIDED THAT OLD
BASKET CHAIR FOR THE COMFORT OF A
WAITING CALLER. AND IS THAT
DAFFODIL SELF-SOWN OR WAS IT
PLANTED TO PROVIDE A LITTLE DASH OF
YELLOW ALONGSIDE THE RED?

Left *Dr. Cox's Garden, Caldbeck, Cumbria*
Above *Greenham, Somerset*

'I HATE TO WORRY YOU, MUMSY, BUT I
THINK I'M GOING TO BE KIDNAPPED.
THERE ARE ALL THESE ODD-LOOKING
PEOPLE IN CARAVANS, AND ONE OF THE
HORSES KEEPS LEERING AT ME. I ALMOST
WISH FREDDIE WAS HERE. . . MUMSY, IF
THEY ASK FOR A RANSOM YOU WILL PAY,
WON'T YOU?'

Gypsies, Conder Green, Near Lancaster

51

Left and above *Matlock Bath, Derbyshire*   **Overleaf, left** *K8, Rhymney, Mid Glamorgan*   **Right** *Grosmont, North Yorkshire*

YOUTH GROUPS

WHO CAN GUESS WHAT DANCE THEY
ARE DANCING AROUND THE K8, OR
WHAT THOUGHTS THEY ARE THINKING
BESIDE THE K6? THE KIOSKS HAVE
PROBABLY BEEN THERE SINCE BEFORE
THEY WERE BORN; IF THE DANCERS
KEEP TO DANCING, AND THE THINKERS
KEEP TO THINKING, THE RED BOXES
WILL SURVIVE THAT MUCH LONGER.

Left *Barrow-in-Furness, Cumbria*
Above *Prestbury, Cheshire*

Left *Kersall, Nottinghamshire*   **Above** *Hammersmith, London*

'Thank goodness, they were only pretend gypsies, and they've given me a lift to the seaside. I can see some children in the distance, showing off in front of a photographer; I'll ask them where I am. Mumsy, are you sure you haven't heard anything from Freddie?'

Left *Seascale, Cumbria*
Overleaf, left *Whitby, North Yorkshire*
Overleaf, right *Robin Hood's Bay, North Yorkshire*

'HALLO, FREDDIE? I JUST HAD TO PHONE YOU. I'M STUCK BY THIS HARBOUR SOMEWHERE TERRIBLY NORTHERN. YES, EVEN NORTH OF WATFORD, BUT I'M SURE YOU CAN FIND IT, FREDDIE, THERE'S A CAFÉ PLACE AND SOME FUNNY LITTLE BOATS AND IT ALL SMELLS OF FISH – YOU REALLY CAN'T MISS IT. DO COME AND TAKE ME HOME, FREDDIE. . .'

Whitby, North Yorkshire

THE UNCROWNED KIOSKS

ONE OF THE EARLIEST TELEPHONE
COMPANIES TO ERECT PUBLIC CALL
OFFICES WAS BASED IN KINGSTON-
UPON-HULL. AT THE TURN OF THE
CENTURY THE NATIONAL TELEPHONE
COMPANY HAD ABSORBED MOST OF ITS
RIVALS, AND IN DUE COURSE THE
N.T.C. WAS TAKEN OVER BY THE POST
OFFICE AND THE POST OFFICE GAVE
PLACE TO BRITISH TELECOM, BUT
THROUGHOUT ALL THE CHANGES HULL
MAINTAINED ITS INDEPENDENCE, AND
ITS OWN KIOSKS. WHICH IS WHY THESE
K6 KIOSKS ARE PAINTED WHITE
INSTEAD OF RED, AND THEY HAVE
NO CROWN TO LINK THEM WITH THE
PUBLIC SERVICE.

Lowgate, Hull

'MUMSY DEAR, YOU ARE JUST NOT GOING TO BELIEVE THIS. YOU KNOW FREDDIE'S BEEN SO SWEET LATELY, SO I SAID I'D GO OUT FOR ANOTHER DRIVE WITH HIM TO SEE HOW THE COUNTRYSIDE LOOKS IN ALL THE SNOW. AND WE STOPPED IN THIS VERY QUIET LITTLE VILLAGE WITH ABSOLUTELY NOBODY ABOUT BECAUSE THEY'RE ALL IN CHURCH, AND WE WERE JUST SITTING HERE LOOKING AT SOME SHEEP, AND MUMSY,

GUESS WHAT FREDDIE DID!!'

Pott Shrigley, Cheshire

Hoylake, Wirral, Merseyside

DEMISE AND RESURRECTION

The Swinging Sixties brought dramatic changes to the British way of life, and the red phone box, which by now was an integral part of it, came under the pressure of change as well. The Jubilee Kiosk had always been square, but now the term had quite a different meaning. Telephone boxes had to get with it . . . man.

There were other criticisms emerging too. The powerfully-sprung door of the kiosk needed a hefty pull, which could be quite beyond the old and frail. Those who did manage it risked their fingernails in the little 'cup' handles. And even with the door open, the disabled might still be unable to reach the telephone.

On the other hand the telephone and its coinbox were all too accessible to thieves and vandals. Our old friend Samuel Wartski was only trying to retrieve his own tuppence when he attacked that phone box in 1907, but in 1921 a man admitted touring kiosks on a motorbike and extracting a steady five or ten pounds a week, and they have been regarded as fair game ever since. By the nineteen-sixties it was estimated that on average every kiosk in Britain was vandalised twice a year.

Various ideas were suggested to protect them. Remote alarms, tougher coinboxes, unbreakable glass – even booby-trapping the box so that if anything was tampered with, the door would lock automatically, penning the miscreant inside. None of them proved practical. The only answer was a new phone box. For the K6 the writing was symbolically as well as literally on the wall.

The first updated kiosk was tried out in the early Sixties. The K7 was designed by Neville Conder on the same lines as the new office blocks which were rising all over London. It had floor-to-ceiling windows with a minimum of metal framework, and what framework it had was aluminium. The glass was on all four sides instead of three, with the telephone in one corner. The 'TELEPHONE' sign which had appeared on the roof of every phone box since 1884 was now considered superfluous and removed.

Alas, like so many products of the early Sixties, the K7 did not stand up to the test of time. Its aluminium body proved quite unsuited to the English climate. The first prototypes were erected in London in January 1962; by the Spring, with the aluminium reduced to what even the Post Office admitted was 'a streaky, grey-black, heavily-blistered mess', it was clear that they were a disaster. Sir Giles Gilbert Scott, who had not lived to see them, must have chuckled quietly in his grave.

Conder, along with two other architects, was invited to try again. Understandably perhaps, he declined. One of the others, whose name confusingly was Scott – he was no relation – apparently had little enthusiasm for the task since he let it be known that he saw nothing much wrong with the well-tried K6. It was the third architect, a pre-fabrication expert called Bruce Martin, who produced the basic design for the K6's eventual successor.

The K8 was something of a compromise between Sir Giles's classical solidity and Conder's ultra-modern airiness. It had big windows, but only on three sides. It did not have a domed roof but it did have the word 'TELEPHONE'. There was not a large area of paintwork, but that paintwork was red. And although Martin wanted it made of aluminium alloy the Post Office, remembering their nasty experience with the 'streaky, grey-black, heavily-blistered mess', decided to stay with cast iron, except for the door.

With his experience of prefabricated buildings Martin designed the kiosk in seven main sections, which could be put together in various ways so the door was opposite the back panel or on either of the two sides, and it could be hinged to open to the left or the right.

The design followed the brief given by the Post Office that it should provide the maximum discouragement to vandals. 'It must be possible to see easily into the kiosk from outside, as a deterrent for miscreants who might attack and rob the fittings and coin box . . . Glazing and fitments must be robust . . . Crevices, into which levers and jemmies could be inserted, must be avoided . . .'

So there was plenty of glass for good visibility, but the glass was toughened to withstand boots and missiles. The back panel had secure fittings to prevent the equipment being ripped away. Wielders of levers and jemmies would not have found a single crevice to prise apart.

A number of other innovative features were incorporated. A gap was left under the door, partly for ventilation, partly to prevent the

Cholmondeley, Cheshire

door being jammed by rubbish or stones. It had the additional effect of providing a brisk draught around the ankles, thus discouraging over-long phone calls.

Fluorescent lighting was installed in place of tungsten lamps, and instead of being operated by a timeswitch during the hours of darkness it was left on all day – which seemed to most of us a very wasteful procedure, but the Tele-Communications Development Department at the Post Office, which knew about these things, said it was actually cheaper.

And there was one other change which was less obvious to the public but had considerable significance in the history of the British telephone box, and gave an indication of how its Britishness would fade. All the dimension of the new kiosk were measured in metric units; it was held together by metric bolts.

The first K8 appeared in London in 1968. It seemed to be as near vandal-proof as man could devise. It did not go streaky or grey-black or blister. It was also much cheaper than the K6, simpler to erect and easier to clean. The Post Office ordered a thousand, then ten thousand more. If one can imagine a 'red box' having a coffin, then the K8 was the first nail in it.

Vandalised Kiosk No. 6, Cheshire

During the next sixteen years, whenever a K6 ended its useful life a K8 was put in its place. The old 'Button B' system was already being phased out before the K8 arrived; now the K6 was being phased out too. In the 1970s the Post Office started experimenting with other variations. To the horror of the purists, though probably no one else noticed, they enlarged the window panes on some of the old K6s. They even tried painting the red box yellow, but not even the ordinary layman would stand for that and they retreated in face of the public outcry. But that was only a temporary reprieve. In 1984 the Post Office was divided and British Telecom was born. The days of the red box were numbered.

It took British Telecom only three months to pronounce the death sentence. All the existing kiosks – not only Scott's but the more recent K8s – were to be removed, regardless of their condition. They would be replaced, not by a universal K9 – how Dr Who would have enjoyed that title being borrowed from his pet robot! – but by an assortment of kiosks, semi-kiosks, booths and head-canopies, based on American and Continental designs. To emphasize they were no longer linked with the Post Office, they would be painted in British Telecom blue and yellow.

When British Telecom made the announcement in January 1985 there were sixty thousand Scott kiosks still in use. In the next four years thirty thousand of them disappeared. Only twelve hundred of the remainder had been granted listed status. But the pace of the purge was slowing. Local councils and communities, noticing the new blue-and-yellow boxes springing up all around them, launched campaigns to save their old ones.

Even in my own little Norfolk village, with a population of under forty, we discussed how we could preserve our ageing K6, for which I have a particular affection. When my telephone was out of action for a week I spent so much time in it that a sympathetic neighbour placed a vase of sweet peas on the coinbox to make it look more homely. We liked to think it was the only kiosk that accepted 5p's, 10p's, and sweet peas . . .

There were some notable victories. In the nearby village of New Buckenham (in Norfolk a village is 'new' unless it goes back beyond the Normans) British Telecom not only agreed to leave the K6 on the village green but completely refurbished it and even picked out the crowns on the roof in gold paint, a remarkable concession. In another Norfolk village, Bawburgh, they installed a new kiosk but agreed to leave the original one beside it, telephone-less, so it could be used as a waiting-room when the new one was occupied! There were other indications, not only in Norfolk, that although Telecom had passed sentence on the red box they might take longer than expected to carry it out. Nonetheless it is still a doomed species; only two-and-a-half thousand, a tiny fraction of the original total, are to be allowed to survive. But as they have become scarcer their rarity value as collectors' items has increased. Ingenious entrepreneurs have been buying up the redundant boxes and devising new uses for them, with an eye to the trans-Atlantic market, where nostalgic ex-colonials are prepared to trans-ship entire cottages and bridges, let alone a modest K6. One catalogue announced:

'For Sale: A little piece of traditional Britain!'
'Regrettable though changes may be, it does provide us with an outstanding opportunity to utilize the box in our homes and gardens in many different and unique ways; ways that make a personal statement about yourself and your values.'

Some of the 'personal statements' which are then

suggested are so bizarre they might give people a very odd idea about yourself and your values. Can you imagine using a Jubilee Kiosk, for example, as a baby-oil dispenser, or a birdcage, or a bubble-machine, or – inevitably – a loo? But the catalogue is perfectly serious. For instance, how about a shower-room?

'A natural for the bathroom or by the pool or both. With just a few adjustments you can have a shower-room, painted to fit in with your colour scheme, that will add value to your property as well as giving you the pleasure of its use . . .'

Or you can remove a few of the glass panels and it becomes a greenhouse, 'an elegant addition to any garden'. Fill it with shelves and you can turn it into a bookcase; install an armchair with a phone extension and 'make it one of the most favourite rooms in the house'.

There is even the K6 Kocktail Kabinet – 'Surely the peak of sophistication and the envy of all who are invited for drinks. Avant-garde? Yes. Over the top? By no means. Perfectly dimensional for this purpose with ample room for fridge, bottle storage and the right height for optics.' And in fact a

Above *Goldthorpe, South Yorkshire*
Right *Goodbye to all that*

76

<u>NOTICE</u>

BRITISH TELECOM WILL SHORTLY BE REPLACING THIS TELEPHONE KIOSK WITH A NEW MODERN ONE.

IN ORDER TO DO THIS, IT WILL BE NECESSARY FOR THE PAYPHONE TO BE TAKEN OUT OF SERVICE FOR A FEW DAYS.

EVERY EFFORT WILL BE MADE TO RESTORE TELEPHONE SERVICE AS QUICKLY AS POSSIBLE.

THE NEAREST ALTERNATIVE PUBLIC CALL BOX IS LOCATED AT:

....

FURTHER INFORMATION CAN BE OBTAINED FROM:-

HOUSING MANAGER REF LP34,
BRITISH TELECOM,
CAMELFORD HOUSE,
87 ALBERT EMBANKMENT,
LONDON.
SE1 7TS

version of the 'K6KK' has already been installed by a hotel in avant-garde Huddersfield; they proudly call it the smallest public bar in Britain.

Ignominious it may seem to a Scott disciple, and Sir Giles himself may well gyrate at the thought of his Jubilee Kiosk being used as a coffee machine or a tumble dryer. But at least it is one form of preservation – and these after all are the lucky ones. In scrapyards all over the country the piles of unwanted kiosks continue to grow, the windows broken, the paint flaked off, the fittings ripped out. If it is any consolation, there will no doubt come a time when the present generation of glossy glass kiosks will meet the same fate. Already an entirely new breed has come into use, the product of Telecom's rival, Mercury Communications. The three different prototypes first appeared on Waterloo Station in July 1988 – and the Thirties Society hated them all.

One was decribed officially by the Mercury designers as a 'communications totem.' Gavin Stamp of the Thirties Society thought it was more like an old-fashioned petrol pump. Another with a glazed canopy he likened to a conservatory. And the third one, which might have pleased his classical eye with its Greek Doric columns, he roundly condemned as 'not only painfully over-elaborate but naively literal . . . The Grecian ornament sits uneasily with the flashy Superman-style Mercury logo.'

There is not, so far as I know, an Eighties Society. If there were, it might well take the view that in the very modern surrounds of Waterloo station the Mercury payphones do not look too out-of-place. And they are already becoming a familiar sight in some of our larger cities, without provoking too many cries of anguish. But this book is not a Prelude for the Pop-Art Payphone but a Requiem for a Red Box, and since Mr Stamp would seem to be the chief mourner let me quote him just one more time for the final benediction.

'The defence of the Scott telephone kiosk was not an exercise in nostalgia, a sentimental protest at yet another change in the public face of Great Britain and at the extinction of a harmless and enjoyable survival from the past . . . The K2s and K6s were not only admirable and efficient as weathertight receptacles for public telephones; they were also supremely excellent models of how sensitive, dignified, and yes, *beautiful* street furniture can be.'

Which is pushing it a bit, but Amen anyway.

Right *Parton, West Cumbria*
Overleaf *Mr. Michael Greene's collection of 26 boxes in the drive of his Oxfordshire home*

Above and left *Binfield Heath, Oxfordshire*

SCOTT FREE

SOON AFTER BRITISH TELECOM WAS
CREATED IN 1984 IT PRONOUNCED THE
DEATH SENTENCE ON THE SCOTT
KIOSKS. THIS ONE SEEMS TO HAVE
ESCAPED OVER THE WIRE, AND LIKE ITS
COMRADES ON THE PREVIOUS PAGE
MAY BE HOPING TO HIDE IN THE TREES,
BUT FOR MOST OF THEM THERE WAS
NO ESCAPE.

Crewton, Allotments, Derby

Left *Harthill, Cheshire*   **Above** *Whitehaven, Cumbria*

Walney Island, Barrow-in-Furness, Cumbria

THE YELLOW SURVIVORS

DURING THE 1970S THE GENERAL POST
OFFICE THOUGH IT MIGHT BE RATHER
JOLLY TO PAINT THEIR TRADITIONAL
RED BOXES YELLOW. THE PUBLIC WAS
ABSOLUTELY INCENSED – OR SO THE
PRESS MAINTAINED – AND THE BOXES
WENT BACK TO RED AGAIN, WITH THE
CURIOUS EXCEPTION OF BARROW-IN-
FURNESS, WHERE WE DISCOVERED
THAT YELLOW K6 PHONE BOXES STILL
SURVIVE. NOBODY SEEMS TO BE QUITE
SURE WHY; IN FACT, THE LOCAL
COUNCIL SEEMED AS SURPRISED BY
THE DISCOVERY AS WE WERE . . .

Above and left *Garstang, Lancashire*

Left *Grange-in-Borrowdale, Cumbria* **Above** *Threlkeld, Cumbria*

Tirril, Cumbria

Isle of Mull, Scotland

THE SPREAD OF THE RED DEATH

FOR FIFTY YEARS TRAVELLERS CAME UPON THE REASSURING PRESENCE OF A SCOTT KIOSK ON FAR-FLUNG SITES LIKE THIS – PERHAPS THE ONLY EVIDENCE OF MAN'S PRESENCE ON A LONELY HILLSIDE OR AN EMPTY VALLEY. THEY OFFERED AT BEST SOME URGENT HELP IN AN EMERGENCY, AT WORST A LITTLE SHELTER FROM THE ELEMENTS. NOW THERE IS JUST A CONCRETE BASE AND A DISCONNECTED WIRE. IN DUE COURSE A SMART, MODERN PAYBOOTH MAY BE INSTALLED INSTEAD – BUT WILL IT EVER BE QUITE THE SAME?

Far left *Shap Summit, Cumbria*
Middle left *Langsleddale, Cumbria*
Left *Langsleddale, Cumbria*

'MUMSY, I'VE BEEN TRYING TO PHONE YOU FROM TWO BOXES IN THIS ROW HERE, BUT SOMEBODY SEEMS TO HAVE TAKEN OUT THE TELEPHONES AND BROKEN SOME OF THE WINDOWS, AND I'VE HAD TO TRY THIS DIFFERENT SORT OF BOX WITH GREAT BIG WINDOWS ALL ROUND IT. I FEEL SO – WELL – EXPOSED, MUMSY. DO YOU THINK I'M ALL RIGHT, STANDING HERE LIKE THIS, OR SHOULD I FIND A PROPER BOX THAT'S STILL GOT A PHONE IN IT?'

Ullapool, Scotland

Left *Galgate, Lancashire*   **Above** *Whitehaven, West Cumbria*

THE GRAVEYARD

IN ITS FIRST FOUR YEARS BRITISH
TELECOM, WIELDING ITS NEW BROOM
LIKE A SCYTHE, FLATTENED THIRTY
THOUSAND TRADITIONAL TELEPHONE
BOXES. THEY WERE CARTED AWAY TO
DEALERS' YARDS TO LIE IN RUSTING
ROWS AMONG THE NETTLES, AWAITING
THE FINAL HUMILIATION OF BEING
REDUCED TO SCRAP METAL.
OCCASIONALLY, A SENTIMENTAL
COLLECTOR CAME TO RESCUE THE ODD
ONE; THEN INGENIOUS ENTREPRENEURS
DISCOVERED THAT A KIOSK BY ANY
OTHER NAME CAN SELL A TREAT. . .
BUT, FOR MANY, IT WAS TOO LATE.

Fyfield, Essex

Above and right *Fyfield, Essex*

Poynton, Cheshire

Poynton, Cheshire

Left *Mr. Robert Ridley, Poynton, Cheshire*   **Above** *Fyfield, Essex*

'YES, MUMSY, IT'S ME AGAIN. I'VE FOUND ONE OF THE OLD BOXES AND IT'S STILL WORKING, BUT THERE ARE SOME MEN OUTSIDE AND THEY SAY THEY WANT TO ALTER SOMETHING. DON'T HANG UP, MUMSY, THEY PROMISE IT WON'T TAKE A MOMENT. . . ARE YOU STILL THERE, MUMSY? THE MEN HAVE GONE NOW BUT THEY'VE TAKEN THAT NICE OLD BOX AWAY AND NOW I'M IN A SORT OF GLASS BOX WITH YELLOW WRITING ON IT AND A CIRCLE WITH DOTS AND THINGS. IT DOESN'T SEEM LIKE A REAL PHONE BOX AT ALL. . .'

Tirril, Cumbria

TELECOM YELLOW

THE NEW BRITISH TELECOM KIOSK.
THE FAMILIAR POST OFFICE RED HAS
BEEN REPLACED BY TELECOM YELLOW
AND INSTEAD OF "TELEPHONE" ON
THE ROOF THERE IS A DOT-DOT-DASH
"T" ON THE GLASS. GRAFFITI ARTISTS
ADAPTED QUICKLY TO THE NEW
COLOUR; THEY FOUND A MATCHING
SHADE OF AEROSOL SPRAY.

Left *Beckfoot, Cumbria*   **Above** *Speke, Liverpool*

*'MUMSY, YOU REMEMBER THAT
DIFFICULT TIME I HAD WITH FREDDIE IN
THE COUNTRY? WELL, WE THOUGHT
WE'D HAVE ANOTHER LITTLE TRIP AND I
SAW THIS FUNNY PHONE BOX SO I
THOUGHT I'D HAVE A CHAT. THERE'S A
LADY WITH SOME DUCKS WHO SAYS SHE
DOESN'T LIKE THE LOOK OF IT BY HER
GATE, BUT I TOLD HER IT LOOKED
RATHER WITH IT, AND SHE SAID WITH
WHAT, SO I GAVE UP.'*

Near Appleby, Cumbria

THE MERCURY EFFECT

MERCURY COMMUNICATIONS, SET UP
TO CHALLENGE THE TELECOM
MONOPOLY IN 1987, PRODUCED ITS OWN
ASSORTMENT OF PHONE BOXES,
RANGING FROM A "COMMUNICATIONS
TOTEM" WITH A FANCY GLASS CANOPY
TO A MORE ORTHODOX BANK OF
PAYBOOTHS. TO CONTRAST WITH
TELECOM YELLOW AND SUPPRESS ANY
MEMORIES OF POST OFFICE RED,
MERCURY PAINTED THEM BLUE – AS IT
HAPPENS, THE COLOUR USED BY THE
NATIONAL TELEPHONE COMPANY
EIGHTY YEARS EARLIER, TO
DISTINGUISH IT FROM ITS RIVALS. NOW
KIOSKS ARE IN COMPETITION AGAIN.

Left *Covent Garden, London*
Right *Waterloo Station, London*

'FREDDIE, ARE YOU QUITE SURE I CAN PHONE MUMSY FROM THIS BOX? I'M SURE IT'S NOT SUPPOSED TO BE LYING ON ITS SIDE LIKE THIS, AND THERE REALLY ISN'T ROOM FOR BOTH OF US IN IT, AND I CAN'T FIND THE PHONE ANYWHERE. AND NOW IT SEEMS TO BE MOVING. . . FREDDIE, STOP IT!'

Near Penrith, Cumbria

Above *Woodford, Greater Manchester*   **Right** *Clungunford, Shropshire*

THE BRAVE NEW WORLD

A SCARLET-UNIFORMED GUARD OF
HONOUR LINES THE DRIVE OF MR.
MICHAEL GREENE'S HOME IN OXFORD-
SHIRE ON PAGES 80 AND 81 – TWENTY-
SIX PENSIONERS SAVED FROM THE
SCRAPHEAP, SOMEWHAT BATTLE-
SCARRED AND NO LONGER FIT FOR
ACTIVE SERVICE, BUT STILL A CREDIT
TO THEIR OLD COMMANDER, SIR GILES
GILBERT SCOTT. HE MIGHT NOT HAVE
BEEN SO HAPPY ABOUT THEIR OTHER
RETIREMENT JOBS, RANGING FROM
COCKTAIL CABINETS TO GARDEN SHEDS,
BUT AT LEAST THEY HAVE ENSURED
THAT THE K6 JUBILEE KIOSK REMAINS
SOMETHING MORE THAN JUST A
MEMORY.

Mr. Willie White's Kiosk No. 6 Kocktail Kabinet
Fyfield Hall, Essex

Mr. and Mrs. John Harrison and family, Bramhall, Cheshire

Yvonne and Alison Hallworth, Davenport Arms, Woodford, Greater Manchester

Left *Paula Ridley and Gemma, Poynton, Cheshire*
Above *Mr. David Hughes with K6 shower cubicle, Alderley Edge, Cheshire*

127

ACKNOWLEDGEMENTS

The photographs are reproduced with
the kind permission of the following:

Neil McAllister 6, 17, 21, 23, 24, 25, 26, 27, 30, 31, 32-3, 34, 35,
36, 38, 40-1, 49, 52, 53, 54, 55, 56-7, 58, 59, 60, 62, 63, 64, 66,
67, 68-9, 70, 73, 74, 76, 77, 80-81, 82, 83, 86, 90, 102-3, 104,
105, 106, 107, 108, 109, 113, 116, 117, 120, 121, 123, 124, 125,
126, 127; Val Corbett 2, 42, 43, 44-5, 46, 47, 48, 56, 87, 88, 89, 92,
93, 94, 95, 96 left and right, 97, 98-9, 101, 110 left and right, 112,
114-5, 118, 128; Isabel Matthews 28, 29, 39, 79, 91; Barbara
Cockburn 50-51, 100; Pete Smith 84-5; Vivian Russell 37; Hulton
Deutch Collection 15 right; Telecom Technology Showcase, 135
Queen Victoria Street, London EC4V 4AT (The British Telecom
Museum) 4, 8, 11 left and right, 12, 13, 15 left, 18, 19

The publishers would like to thank
Mr. Willie White of Pilot Developments, Fyfield, Essex

Commissioning Editor Trevor Dolby
Design Alyson Kyles
Design Assistant Sarah Pollock
Picture Research Gail Carlill
Production Claire Kane

The author would like to acknowledge:
'Britain's Public Payphones', published by British Telecom, and other
GPO and Telecom publications.
Telecom Showcase and its Curator, Neil Johanson.
'Telephone Boxes' and 'The Battle of the Phone Booth' by Gavin Stamp.
Breckland District Council Planning Department.
The neighbour who put flowers in our village kiosk to make it more
homely during the week my own phone was out of order . . .
. . . and the telephone engineer who finally put it right.